808.7 Bee   4334
BEE   In spite of everything!

In spite of

everything!

History of the State of Israel
in political cartoons

by Noah Bee

Edited by
Ernest E. Barbarash

BLOCH PUBLISHING COMPANY

New York

To my dear wife
Marian
for her patience, understanding
and help in
bringing this project
into reality

International Standard Book No. 0-8197-0297-8
Library of Congress Catalogue Card No. 73-77-304
Copyright © Noah M. Bee
Printed in the United States of America

Foreword

Twenty-five years is a very brief period in history. But this short span of time since the establishment of the State of Israel makes up for 1,900 years of the Jewish Dispersion. Since 70 A.D. the Jewish people have been subjected to a succession of exiles, pogroms, persecutions, and ultimately to the gas chambers. The founding of Israel changed the status of the Jew. He became the master of his own destiny.

The events of the past twenty-five years have been full of progress, dynamism, and guts. They were most exhilarating and fascinating experiences to observe from the top of the drawing board, and afforded a unique opportunity to report and interpret in satire, symbol, and caricature all those significant moments as they made up the pattern of history.

It all started on that fateful Friday, May 14, 1948, when the little man with the bushy white hair announced that the new state was to be called 'Israel'. The first round of the War of Liberation against the Arabs was over, and the people began to move toward consolidating their newly won freedom. A few peaceful years followed with only sporadic shooting on the borders; years of recognition, diplomacy, and economic struggle. The overthrow of King Farouk of Egypt and the rise of Abdel Gamal Nasser, a new symbol of Arab aspirations, brought a change to the Middle East. Besides his talent for stirring up the masses, he was a blessing to the cartoonist. His imposing posture, bull neck, and eagle nose soon became a popular symbol of his image and remained the center of attention until his death. The Suez crisis in 1956, and subsequent developments propelled Israel into the world arena as a dominant force in that strategic area.

The years that followed saw an increasing struggle marked by political maneuvers and alignments in the United Nations. The Soviet Bear moved down from the cold North into the South, and encamped on the warm sands of Egypt. The Sphinx assumed a different face. The Middle East volcano was growing hotter, and the war drums beat louder and louder. Little Israel braced itself for the fateful days of conflict. When they arrived, she acted with tremendous impact and speed. The magic carpet was pulled from under Nasser and the Soviet Bear lost face. The world was astounded; some were stunned, some resentful, but the facts spoke louder than words. The third round was over in six days—and at nineteen Israel had come of age.

The Eshkol years drew to a close and the Golden Age dawned with Golda. Politically, Israel turned a corner at LBJ and Nixon Avenues. The Soviets kept the extremists in Cairo in check by dangling a carrot on a stick in front of them. Nasser's heir, Sadat, inherited a mess, but fantasy still permeated Arab thinking. With characteristic Levantine fervor, he maneuvered, yelled, threatened, and set deadlines until the ground began to sink under him. Then the big bombshell fell. Russki out! But are they really out?

Terrorism and hijacking became the only "art" the Arab foes managed to master. But that scored no gains and forfeited sympathy. Nothing really changed save the growing anti-Israel bloc at the U.N. There they succeeded in gaining in the war of public relations. The lofty ideals of the World Organization were slowly buried under the East River in New York.

Who knows what the future holds? But one certainty does stand out—Israel has survived its first twenty-five years, and what years they have been!

In the meantime, the eye of the cartoonist is always on the lookout for a new face, new situations, or new symbol, ready to dip his brush into the ink and make a modest contribution to the march of history.

—Noah Bee

May 1973 (25th Anniversary of the State of Israel)

World War II came to an end with six million Jews slaughtered and no place for those who had survived. The only possible home was in Palestine, but its doors were locked. The British continued to appease the Arabs. In an attempt to cope with the problem a joint Anglo-American Fact Finding Committee was formed.

The new world promised by the victorious Allies seemingly included everyone except those who had suffered the most. The British tried to sidetrack the pledges for the establishment of a Jewish National Home in Palestine. President Harry S. Truman urged the admission of 100,000 Jewish refugees, but his plea was rejected. Finally on November 29, 1947, the United Nations General Assembly voted for the partition of Palestine. The Jews accepted but the Arabs rejected it.

The British continued their iron rule, and attempts of the homeless Jews to reach the Promised Land were crushed with very few exceptions. A dramatic symbol of this struggle was the ship "Exodus 1947", which was intercepted as it neared Palestine with an overload of 4,400 refugees. Foreign Minister Bevin ordered the human cargo returned to the Displaced Persons camps in Germany. Resistance to British policy had gained momentum, led by the Haganah, the Irgun, and the more extremist Stern gang, bringing the country near paralysis. The British, unnerved and weary, decided to quit. And in February, 1947, they threw the problem into the lap of the United Nations.

In spite of everything ...

May 14, 1948. This day marked the beginning of a new era in the history of the Jewish people. The long road of the Dispersion had come to an end. The cane and knapsack, which had symbolized the wandering Jew, were discarded. The British High Commissioner departed in the morning, bringing to an end the twenty-eight years of British rule. In the afternoon, on the eve of the Sabbath, the National Council representing all elements of the Jewish Community gathered in Tel Aviv to hear David Ben-Gurion proclaim the birth of M'dinat Israel.

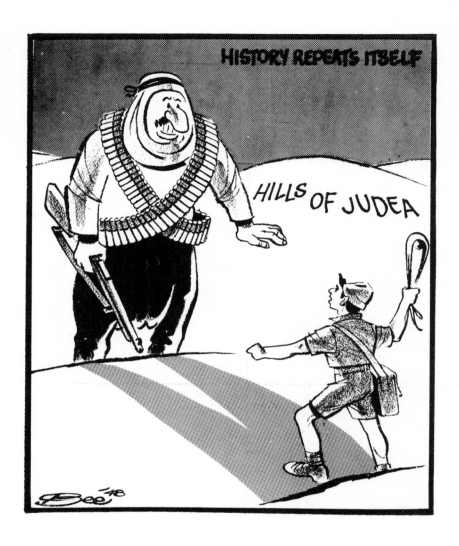

The new state found itself at war with five Arab countries on the first day of its existence. The Haganah, officially renamed the Defense Army of Israel, could barely muster 25,000 men and women armed with obsolete weapons. With valor and spirit the invaders were repelled.

On May 14, 1948, eleven minutes after the proclamation of the State of Israel, President Harry S. Truman announced de facto recognition of the state. The Soviet Union shortly thereafter extended its recognition followed by many other countries.

The first Government embraced a broad coalition of all major parties from the Socialist left to the Orthodox right. Mapai, the largest Labor party, comprised the majority of the Cabinet. Conscious of Israel's new role in the international arena, particularly in its relations with the United States and American Jewry, the new government steered a middle course in its economic and political policies.

The siege and liberation of Jerusalem constituted the most memorable chapters of the War of Independence. With the city cut off, the powerful Transjordanian Arab Legion had succeeded in occupying the Jewish quarter in the Old City. The 90,000 Jews faced starvation, but they held out gallantly until June 11, 1948, when a breakthrough took place via a secretly built road.

While negotiations were underway for a ceasefire agreement with the Arab States, British Foreign Secretary Bevin maneuvered to sever the Negev from the state's tiny territory. President Truman's firm stand frustrated Bevin's schemes.

After a truce was established on June 11, 1948, by the United Nations, the Israelis strengthened their military and economic position. An armistice agreement was signed with Egypt on February 2, 1949, on Rhodes, ending the first round of warfare.

Encouraged by their leaders to abandon their homes, in spite of pleas by the Israeli authorities, Arabs fled during the War of Liberation. They heeded the stories of atrocities, and promises of acquiring Jewish property after Arab victory. Their rulers then dumped the refugee problem on the doorstep of the United Nations.

As Israel busied herself with building up its social, political, and economic life and strengthened the security of its borders, the Arab masses in the neighboring countries were seething with rage and frustration. The unfulfilled promises of victories by their rulers resulted in turmoil and discontent.

Although the Arab states signed ceasefire agreements, they would not accept the existence of the State. Their diplomats toured world capitals and worked strenuously within the United Nations to block the admission of Israel as a member of the world body.

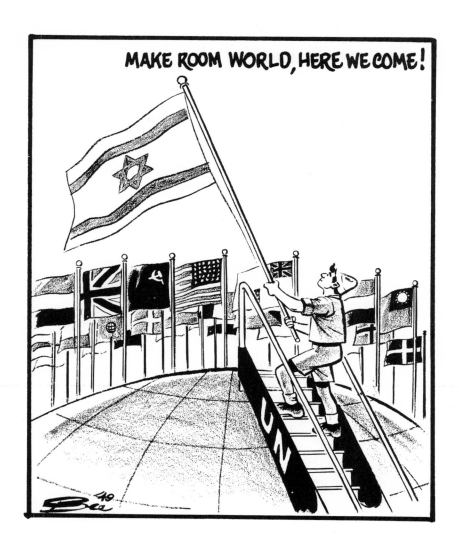

On May 11, 1949, the State was admitted as the 59th member of the United Nations. It was a historic moment when Foreign Minister Moshe Sharett and Ambassador Abba Eban took their seats at Lake Success.

Symbolizing the age old dream of freedom in Zion Reborn, Dr. Chaim Weizmann was elected the first President of Israel. The man largely responsible for the Balfour Declaration, the charter of the Jewish National Home, took his oath of office at the Knesset in Jerusalem on February 14, 1949.

A FAIRY TALE COME TO LIFE

The Biblical prophecy of the Return from Exile was being fulfilled in 1950 when the entire Jewish population of Yemen—45,000 people—was flown to Israel under operation "Magic Carpet." This exodus was followed a year later by another gigantic airlift of 123,000 emigrants from Iraq, virtually bringing to an end the oldest Jewish exile.

It was President Truman's conviction that economic development of Israel would benefit the entire Middle East. Under His Point IV program for technical assistance, the U.S., toward the end of 1951, granted Israel 65 million dollars as part of its aid program for the Middle East and Africa.

Israel marked her fourth anniversary in May, 1952. Despite hardships faced by the country, she celebrated her birthday with a clean bill of health. Laws were passed for the encouragement of foreign investment, accompanied by a drive for increased productivity and stabilization of prices.

The constant feuds among Arab factions, which reached a crescendo in 1952, afforded Israel a breathing spell. Maintaining vigilance, the country proceeded to catch up on the building of homes for the stream of thousands of newcomers and the expansion of its economy.

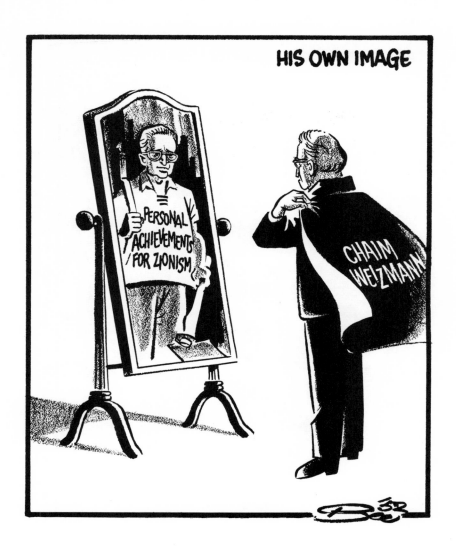

HIS OWN IMAGE

The first President's term of office drew to a close on November 19, 1951, under rules prescribed by the first Knesset. Dr. Weizmann was elected for an extended five year term, but he died on November 9, 1952. Itzhak Ben-Zvi was elected to succeed him.

The approach of Passover in 1952 saw an accelerated tempo in the mobilization of world Jewry to further Israel's economic development. This took the form of launching a one billion dollar loan (Israel Bonds), plus United Jewish Appeal funds to aid Israel's heavy burdens of immigrant absorption.

Iraq, which supported the Axis in World War II, was one of the Arab states that invaded Israel in 1948. The State Department in 1954 furnished Iraq with arms intended for defense against Soviet aggression.

Unmarried women aged 18 to 26 are required to serve in the defense forces for two years. They serve as non-combatant personnel. The ultra-orthodox Neturei Karta protested against recruitment of women as a violation of their interpretation of religious laws.

A double standard was applied by the Big Powers in the United Nations, condemning Israeli defensive acts while ignoring Arab terrorist attacks on Israeli civilians. In March, 1954, a busload of school children was waylaid in the Negev and 19 were massacred. Not a word of reprimand was uttered.

Increasing dissatisfaction with the corrupt rule of King Farouk led to a coup on July 23, 1952, by a group of colonels, naming General Naguib President. However, a new leader emerged, Gamal Abdel Nasser, who assumed the top post on November 14, 1952. With the help of the State Department, the dictator of the Nile was built up as the leader of the Arab Middle East.

The hand of peace, which Israel repeatedly extended, was flatly rejected by the Arabs. In 1954, following international treaties involving England, France and the U.S., the Arab rulers stated that "there will be no peace and no negotiations." This was accompanied by a declaration by Syria's Premier Khoury that a second round is in the making.

The Arab States, led by Egypt, feigned support of the West while cuddling up to Russia. The State Department under John Foster Dulles in 1954 increased the shipments of arms to the Arabs but responded to Israel's pleas for arms with promises.

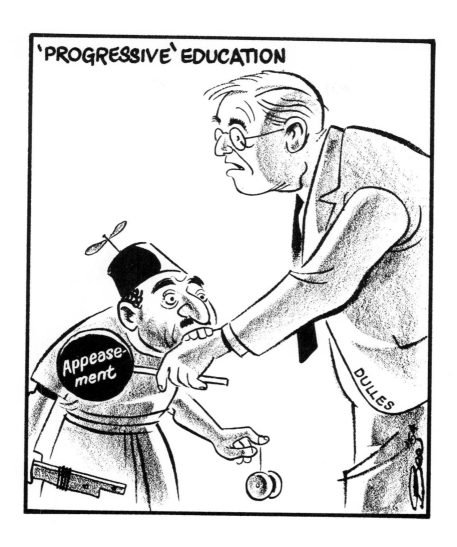

Secretary of State Dulles' attempts to appease the Arabs with financial and arms aid as part of his Cold War strategy did not dissuade the Arab rulers from denouncing the U.S. at every opportunity and at the same time playing up to the Soviets.

HAZARDS OF PLAYING WITH FIRE...

With the Middle East a tinder box as a result of Egypt's blocking Israeli ships from entry into Eilat, the State Department continued in 1955 its policy of furnishing arms to Iraq and Syria. Well-armed Arab terrorist bands launched intensified attacks on settlements in Israel.

Late 1955 saw renewed Egyptian infiltration along the Gaza Strip and similar action by Arab bands into other Israeli areas. Foreign Minister Moshe Sharett pursued a policy of restraint in the hope of a settlement. It was fruitless.

During the latter part of 1954, the State was racked by controversy due to an unsuccessful Israeli intelligence operation in Egypt, which became known as the "Lavon Affair," after Defense Minister Pinchas Lavon, who was blamed for the fiasco by Ben-Gurion.

A Czechoslovakian deal with Egypt in 1955 supplied the Arab countries with sophisticated armaments, placing Israel in peril. Egypt's game of playing Russia and the U.S. against each other resulted in her receiving more American arms.

Egypt violated the international law in 1951 by banning Israel navigation through the Suez Canal. Nasser went further on July 26, 1956, when he announced his decision to nationalize the Canal. This was in line with his goal of gaining hegemony over the Arab Middle East.

On October 29, 1956, Israel's forces, in coordination with the British and French, invaded Egypt. Led by Major General Moshe Dayan, they fought their way through the Sinai Desert at lightning speed and reached the Suez Canal. On November 6, a ceasefire was accepted and a U.N. force was dispatched.

ROCK OF AGES

ASIAN-AFRICAN DEMAND FOR SANCTIONS

ISRAEL

Israel insisted on her legal right to free passage through the Gulf of Aqaba as a condition for her withdrawal from Sinai. In February, 1957, the Asian-African bloc in the U.N. General Assembly tried to invoke sanctions against Israel. However, relying upon President Eisenhower's assurance that the U.S. would assure free passage, Israel withdrew her forces.

The freedom of navigation in the Gulf, made possible by the Sinai campaign, stimulated rapid development of the Negev. The port of Eilat was the sieve for the docking of many ships, tankers and the loading of Israeli products destined for Asia and East Africa.

Russia's long-standing goal dating from Czarist days of gaining a foothold in the Middle East moved ahead when Syria made a request to the Kremlin in 1957 for economic aid, and later for military assistance.

The Baghdad pact was signed in 1957 as a part of the Eisenhower Doctrine, which was designed to serve as a deterrent against Soviet expansion. This prompted the U.S. to restrain Israel from retaliating to almost daily intrusions across its borders. However, the U.S. policy did not succeed, and the pact went into limbo.

On February 28, 1958, David Ben-Gurion, in an interview published in Look magazine, made overtures to Nasser, declaring that if invited, he would visit Cairo. The Israeli Prime Minister made it clear that he would be ready to sign peace treaties with the Arabs if given terms of equality.

The stream of arms flowing to the Arab States from the U.S. and Russia in 1958 threatened to place Israel at a serious disadvantage. In response to urgent pleas for military support, the U.S. advised Israel to turn to NATO. The outcome was negative.

In 1958, formation of the United Arab Republic was announced, merging Egypt and Syria. The move was attributed to Nasser's fear of the Communists in Syria becoming too strong and posing a threat to his ambitions.

IN THE SHADOW OF THE SOVIET SPHINX

Russian influence in the Middle East grew immensely as the Communist leaders threw their support behind the Arabs. The Russians sided with the Arabs at every opportunity in the U.N., despite their unprovoked attacks on Israeli settlements. Kruschev began to take on the image of the Great Protector in the eyes of the Arab states.

U.S. economic aid to Arab countries soared in 1959, while grants to Israel ended after 1957. Thereafter, aid to Israel consisted largely of loans and surplus food.

Shortly after the overthrow of the Iraqi monarchy in July of 1958 by a coup initiated by General Abdul Kassim, quarrels took place between the new Iraqi Premier and President Nasser. In the course of the mutual recriminations, the Egyptian dictator charged that Iraq was selling out to Communism.

Israel protested the U.N.'s failure to enforce passage rights through the Canal. Egypt repeatedly halted freighters heading to or from Israel, and had their cargoes confiscated. On May 22, 1957, Israeli patrol boats seized an Egyptian freighter, the Abdul Karim, bound for Lebanon, and confiscated it.

The State held general elections to the Fourth Knesset on November 3, 1959. Out of 1,219,000 eligible voters, close to one million cast ballots, two-and-one-half times the number voting in the first elections. A Coalition Government was formed, with David Ben-Gurion as Prime Minister.

In the post-Stalin era, with the Russian government led by Kruschev, the Big Four Powers were set to hold a Summit meeting in June of 1960. The Middle East situation loomed on the horizon as Nasser kept threatening another round of war. The meeting was aborted by the U-2 incident.

The independence won by the African states from the British and French colonial rule confronted those countries with serious economic problems. Israel was among the first to offer technical aid.

The increasingly tight blockade by Egypt against Israeli bound shipping aggravated the Suez crisis. The United Nations was indulging in endless futile debates. Secretary General Dag Hammarskjold sought to involve the three Big Powers in the issue.

As the State of Israel turned 13, attaining the traditional Bar Mitzvah age, the country made dramatic progress in every sphere—industrial, agricultural and social. The milestone was marked by an outpouring of solidarity from Jewry the world over.

In May of 1960, the world learned of the capture of Adolf Eichmann in Argentina, a top Nazi criminal involved in the slaughter of six million Jews. After a lengthy trial, and mountainous evidence of his role in carrying out Hitler's "final solution," Eichmann was sentenced to death. He was executed on May 31, 1962.

On September 28, 1961, a coup by the Syrian army led to the dissolution of the United Arab Republic. Syria had resented finding itself the junior partner in the merger, and opposed Egypt's economic policies.

The creation in 1958 of the European Common Market (Euromart) consisting originally of six countries to promote free movement of trade threatened to isolate Israel from its logical share of the European market. Four years after the formation of Euromart, Israel began enlisting the cooperation of its members in obtaining assurances of non-discrimination.

President Nasser's attempt to create Arab unity under his tutelage by the formation of a new Arab Federation in 1963 proved ineffectual, as the rivalries between Arab leaders continued. Nasser was aware that he would stand alone in launching a new war.

THE NEW PILOT

ISRAEL

ESHKOL

On June 24, 1963, Levi Eshkol, Finance Minister, took over the helm of the Government, replacing David Ben-Gurion. His first pronouncement was an appeal to the Great Powers to prevent an arms imbalance in the Mideast, accompanied by a pledge to pursue his efforts for peace.

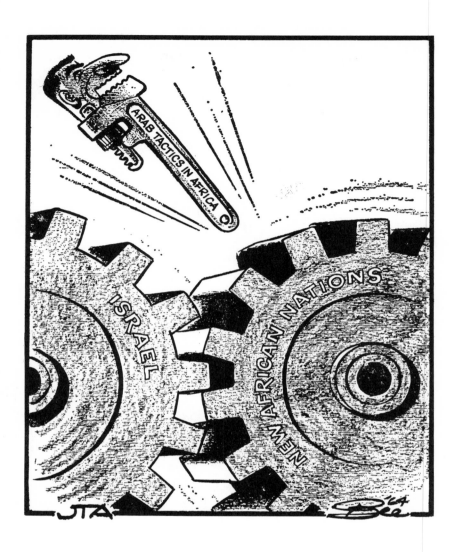

By 1964, the State had established friendly relations with most African countries, many of which sent students to Israel for agricultural and technical training. Arab States sought to sever these ties of friendship by accusing Israel of serving as an agent of Western imperialism.

The advent of 1964 saw a continuation of the vociferous campaign by Egypt to spread anti-Israel propaganda throughout the world. The effort to mobilize world opinion against the state met with only limited success.

King Hussein of Jordan, a junior member of the Arab bloc, reconciled with Nasser during a 1964 summit meeting in Cairo. This prompted the Jordanian leader to emulate the tactics of his "big brother," by intimating to the West that he would join the so-called non-aligned group of Asian and African nations.

President Nasser's charisma in the Arab world, his chief attribute, encouraged him to show off his power to convert the vast economic aid granted by the United States into arsenals for use against the Jewish State.

The refugees were used as pawns by Arab rulers in rallying support in the United Nations against Israel. The Arabs who fled in 1948 at the urging of the invaders were forced to remain in the refugee camps. Their resettlement in neighboring Arab states, most of which were under-populated, was barred.

In 1964, Israel uncovered the presence in Egypt of many Nazi scientists busily engaged in secret military production. Most of them carried West German passports, and were hired at huge fees.

The year 1964 saw an intensified terrorist campaign. Infiltrators, organized and trained in Egypt and Syria, attacked settlements along the border. These bands operated under the name of Palestine Liberation Organization headed by Ahmed Shukeiry.

Following his visit to Arab countries in 1965, President Habib Bourguiba of Tunisia called for Mideast peace negotiations. He accused Nasser of demagoguery but his urging of co-existence aroused the ire of Arab leaders.

On July 7, 1965, the State mourned the death of Moshe Sharett, one of the signers of the Proclamation of Independence on May 14, 1948. An advocate of moderation, he served as Foreign Minister, and in 1954, as Prime Minister.

The country's democracy in action was again demonstrated on November 2, 1965, when 1,244,706 people went to the polls to vote for members of the Sixth Knesset. David Ben-Gurion, delivered the opening address. "We are a people like all other people, but our resurgence, our continued existence and our historic tasks are unique in the annals of mankind," he said.

On May 12, 1965, two decades after the end of World War II, the establishment of diplomatic relations between West Germany and Israel was announced. No Jew could ever forget the holocaust, but this historic move was a recognition that the time was ripe to move on to a new official relationship.

SABRE DANCE

SOVIET ARMS

The massive flow of Soviet arms into Egypt, accompanied by military "advisers," accelerated the Russification of U.A.R.'s military apparatus. President Nasser visited Moscow, and was praised by high Soviet officials as the true leader of the Arabs.

At the meeting of the General Assembly of the United Nations in 1965, Foreign Minister Golda Meir again made a fervent appeal for peace with the Arabs. She pleaded with them to "substitute the doctrine of war with a doctrine of fruitful cooperation."

On January 12, 1966, Levi Eshkol formed an 18 member coalition cabinet comprised of the Labor Alignment, National Religious Front, Mapam, Independent Liberals and Poale Agudath Israel. Abba Eban replaced Golda Meir as Foreign Minister of the Jewish State.

Arriving in New York in March, 1966, on a state visit, King Faisal of Saudi Arabia was snubbed by City and State officials when he made gratuitous comments about Jews. His statement that "we consider those Jews who provide assistance to our enemies as our enemies" was regarded as offensive.

In May, 1966, Soviet Premier Aleksei Kosygin visited Cairo and sharply assailed Israel as an imperialist aggressor and as a country engaged in provocation. He urged the "progressive" Arab countries like Egypt, Syria and Iraq to form a united front in the Middle East.

Following diplomatic relations, an economic accord was signed in Bonn on May 12, 1966, under which West Germany agreed to extend Israel 37½ million dollars in credit. This was part of a trade program and did not represent an extension of reparation payments.

On June 17, 1966, Zalman Shazar, the third President of Israel, embarked on a good will mission to Argentina, Brazil, Uruguay and Chile. The President was accorded a warm welcome and enthusiastic throngs demonstrated their friendship for the people of Israel.

In 1966 Israel's economy, burdened by massive defense and immigrant absorption outlays, underwent a spiraling inflation. The population responded to the needs of the hour by voluntary wage cuts and increased productivity.

Even as the Soviet Union professed at the Security Council its desire for peace, Syrian marauders, heavily armed with Soviet weapons, continued to attack Jewish settlements. This provoked retaliation by striking at the terrorist base at Es-Samu, Jordan, in November, 1966.

On September 22, 1966, the General Assembly of the United Nations convened in the shadow of increasing tensions in the Middle East. The sessions were filled with seemingly endless anti-Israel debates by the pro-Arab bloc backed by the Soviet Union. Pleas for negotiations and an end to infiltrations were ignored.

THE WARP AND THE WOOF

David Ben-Gurion, the architect of the State, marked his eightieth birthday on October 16, 1966. Called the Lion of Zion, he more than any other leader shaped the pattern of the nation's society.

THE CHAIRMAN IS ABOUT TO PLUNGE

MIDDLE EAST TROUBLE

Communist China was vying with Soviet Russia in ingratiating herself with the Arabs. This was motivated by its bitter territorial conflict with Soviet Russia, which was reportedly maintaining a million troops at Manchuria. Cairo disclosed on November, 1966, that Arab terrorists have been receiving arms and training in China.

With a trade deficit in 1966 of 445 million dollars, the Government enacted laws designed to avert a serious depletion in the foreign currency reserves for essential raw material imports.

As the build-up of Egyptian troops in Sinai was under way in May, 1967, the Arab rulers began broadcasting blood-curdling calls in Cairo, Damascus and Baghdad promising "total war" for the "final extermination and annihilation of Israel from the face of the earth." They summoned the Arab people to join in the "most holy campaign."

Tensions in the Middle East mounted early in May, 1967, when Soviet officials claimed that a huge Israeli military buildup along the Syrian frontier was taking place. Eshkol issued a strong denial and invited the Soviet Ambassador to inspect the border area, but the offer was rejected.

On May 18, 1967, Nasser demanded the withdrawal of the United Nations peace keeping force from Sinai and the Gaza Strip. Secretary General U Thant promptly complied. Egyptian troops then proceeded to occupy positions at Sharm el-Sheikh and closed the Straits of Tiran to Israeli shipping.

On Monday, June 5, 1967, war erupted with Egypt. The waiting game was over. The Israeli Defense Force (Zahal) raced into the Sinai desert, and within hours the outcome was sealed. The Egyptian Air Force was destroyed, which left its army without cover. Advance forces reached Suez on June 7, ending the lightning campaign on that front.

The daring sweep through the Sinai enabled the Zahal to turn to the eastern front. Following fierce battles with Jordanian Army units in the Jerusalem area, Zahal forces reached the Western Wall on June 6. The victory fulfilled a 2,000 year old dream of the Jewish people. The Wall is the most sacred site of the Jews since the Temple was destroyed in 70 AD by the Romans. Jerusalem was again reunified.

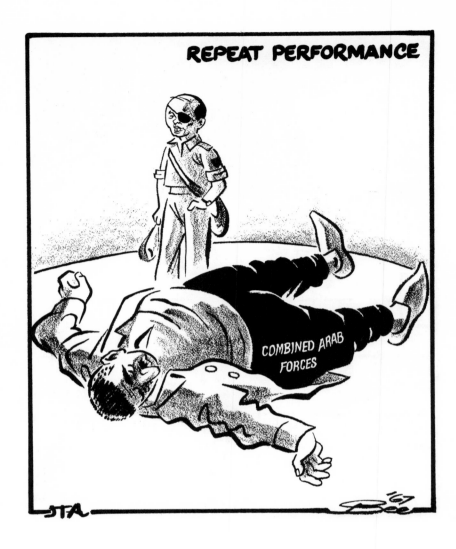

With the defeat of the Syrian Army and occupation of the heavily fortified Golan Heights the Six-Day War came to an end. Israel scored a brilliant victory, thanks to the spirit of its people, and the skill of its military forces under the leadership of Defense Minister Moshe Dayan.

At the outbreak of the Six-Day War, Israel once more stood alone among the "family" of nations. Its only ally in the battle for survival was world Jewry. After the dramatic triumph over the aggressors, an unprecedented outpouring of solidarity and financial support from the Jews the world over took place.

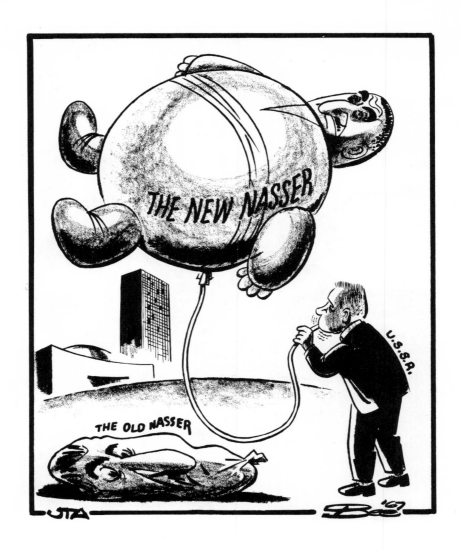

Following the war and a hot-line exchange with President Johnson, in which the U.S. leader warned the Russians to keep their forces at arm's length, Kosygin came to the U.N., where he again called Israel an aggressor. In July, 1967, U.S.S.R. President Podgorny rushed to Cairo and promised Nasser arms to replace the massive losses in the war. He kept that pledge.

On July 2, 1967, Israel announced it would permit Arab refugees who fled during that war to return to their homes. This move was in sharp contrast to the brutal treatment of the Jewish remnants in Arab States.

Following their crushing defeat, Arab rulers held a summit meeting in Khartoum on August 29, 1967, and adopted a resolution calling for the withdrawal of "aggressor forces," and took the position of "no peace with Israel, no negotiations with Israel, no recognition of Israel," one which is in force to this very day.

The Security Council on October 25, 1967, adopted a resolution
calling on Egypt and Israel to "cease immediately" all military
operations. Both the U.S. and U.S.S.R. were anxious to avoid a wider
conflagration in that area.

At a press conference on November 27, 1967, President Charles de Gaulle of France delivered a lengthy discourse on Israel, the Jewish people and the Six Day War. He made comments unfriendly to the Jews and Israel. The old General resented the failure of Israel to follow his advice of "restraint." His position marked the end of the unofficial but close alliance of the two governments.

92

On October 12, 1967, forty-three crewmen were killed and forty-eight wounded when the Israeli destroyer Elath was sunk in the Mediterranean by an Egyptian warship equipped with Russian missiles.

It all started with a letter written on November 2, 1917, by Arthur James Balfour, British Foreign Secretary, to Lord Lionel Rothschild pledging that His Majesty's Government would facilitate the establishment of a Jewish National Home in Palestine. The Balfour Declaration was incorporated in the Mandate entrusted to Britain by the League of Nations.

94

The dawn of the new year 1968 brought into focus the continued penetration of the Kremlin into the Middle East through large-scale arms shipments to Egypt, Syria and Iraq. Nevertheless there was some hope that the Soviets might create a better atmosphere for peace.

The large Arab population, including those in refugee camps, living in areas administered by Israeli forces, posed a major problem for the state. The country had to provide them with employment, housing, social welfare and health services. Appeals to the United Nations in February, 1968, for assistance fell on deaf ears.

Prime Minister Eshkol conferred with President Johnson at his ranch in Texas on January 7 and 8, 1968. Following the meeting, an agreement to supply Phantom jets to offset the heavy Soviet arms shipments to Egypt was signed.

Reversing its policy of friendship towards Israel, France agreed on April 6, 1968, to sell Iraq 54 Mirage supersonic fighter-bombers. There were reports of arms deals with other Arab states.

Ambassador Gunnar Jarring in November, 1967, was named as mediator under resolution of the Security Council in an effort to achieve a peace agreement. During June and July, 1968,he met with Egyptian and Israeli diplomats in London, but Egypt rejected all "proximity" talks.

In 1968 the Soviet stepped up its shipments of weapons to Egypt to replenish losses in the Six-Day War. The number of Soviet warships increased suddenly in the eastern Mediterranean and created a threat to the American Sixth Fleet.

Negotiations which opened in Paris in 1968 to bring to an end the war in Vietnam were cited as an example for the Middle East. Even though negligible progress was reported initially, the talks drew attention to repeated offers to the Arabs to sit down and negotiate.

The West Bank was the scene of constant clashes between the Israeli Army and terrorists infiltrating from Jordan. On March 21, 1968, 15,000 troops crossed into Jordan and attacked their bases. When the incursions continued, air and ground raids in August destroyed additional terrorist centers.

Russia's invasion of Czechoslovakia in 1968 and occupation of that country lent an ironic twist to repeated charges leveled by Soviet leaders against Israeli "aggression."

The U.N. continued its policy of condemning Israel's reactions to Arab terrorism. On August 16, 1968, the Security Council adopted a resolution censuring that country for its air raid on bases near Salt, deep inside Jordan.

King Hussein supported the aims of the terrorists based in his country, but wanted them to submit to his command. After a confrontation in November, 1968, a seven-point pact was concluded ironing out relations between them.

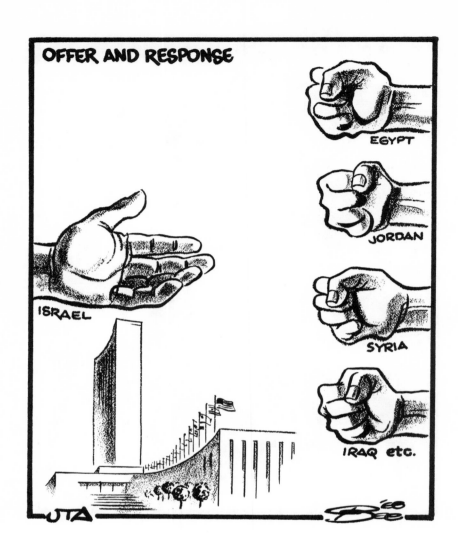

A 9-point peace plan was presented to the General Assembly on October 8, 1968, by Israel's Foreign Minister Abba Eban. It called for secure boundaries, a non-aggression pact, open frontiers, freedom of navigation and a solution to the refugee problem.

Israelis were keenly interested in the U.S. election campaign of 1968. Although both parties reaffirmed support for the state, reliance on America made them highly sensitive to anything which would tend to weaken these ties.

Arab League leaders continued, as the year 1968 drew to a close, to predict renewed round of war. They demanded not only withdrawal to the pre-1967 armistice lines, but urged return to the partition lines of 1947 which were abolished by their invasion after the birth of the State.

Helicopter-borne commandoes swooped down on Beirut International Airport on December 28, 1968, and destroyed 13 empty Arab airliners. The move was in response to a terrorist attack on an El-Al jet in Athens two days earlier. Predictably, the Security Council again censured Israel.

The embargo imposed by DeGaulle on the sale of arms to France's former ally, plus cancellation of the order for 50 Mirages already paid for, constituted a serious blow. On January 14, 1969, Premier Levi Eshkol expressed his distress before the Knesset, but vowed to find new sources of supply and to develop Israel's own weapons capacity.

The Soviets circulated a "peace" plan requiring withdrawal from all territory gained during the Six-Day War. The proposal called for setting up a buffer zone patrolled by U.N. troops and the depositing of a document ending 20 years of war. The Straits of Tiran were to remain open to Israeli shipping, but passage through the Suez Canal was not mentioned.

Jews remaining in Iraq, estimated at 3,000, were subjected to mistreatment and charged with "collaborating with Zionism." In February, 1969, nine Jews were among those hanged publicly as alleged spies. This act aroused revulsion throughout the world.

On February 26, 1969, Levi Eshkol died of a heart attack. On March 17, 1969, Golda Meir succeeded him as Prime Minister. Eshkol's major contribution to the Jewish State was his leadership during the Six-Day War. After much hesitation, brought about by a desire for a peaceful resolution of the conflict, armed forces under his government achieved one of the greatest victories in history.

With the approach of Spring, 1969, Arab bands became bolder and
again struck civilian settlements. With encouragement from Egypt,
they committed acts of destruction, but complaints lodged with the
U.N. went unheeded.

On March 24, 1969, Washington announced that talks had been taking place between Britain, France, the U.S.S.R. and the U.S. on a settlement in the Mideast. Since the Russians and the French were committed to all-out support of the Arabs, and the British were lukewarm, the U.S. alone was in a position to prevent an imposed settlement.

May 1969, saw the surfacing of forces on the American scene supporting the Arab guerilla groups in their acts of aggression. These forces embraced Arab student groups, the Radical New Left and Black extremists espousing the cause of el-Fatah.

In 1969, Egypt escalated its War of Attrition and inflicted an alarming number of casualties among the Israelis. This impelled fortification of the Sinai defenses by building the Bar-Lev line, named for Zahal's Chief of Staff.

Ambassador Jarring's efforts as mediator encountered difficulties as a result of the Arabs' refusal to negotiate unless Israel withdraws first from "every inch" of territory, and return to the old armistice lines. This led U.N. Secretary General U-Thant to announce on May 14, 1969, a temporary suspension of his mission.

Summer, 1969, saw an upsurge of tourism to Israel. Jews from the U.S. and Europe flocked to see the land, and large numbers of Christians came to visit the shrines. Tourism had become a major source of revenue for the state.

Throughout the Summer of 1969, Nasser continued his War of Attrition designed to wear Israel out by constant ground and air bombings across the Suez. He claimed in a speech before the Arab Socialist Union that the "stage was approaching for the liberation of our land."

120

Prime Minister Meir's visit to the White House in September, 1969, focused attention on her country's dependence upon American military and economic aid. She reiterated her desire for negotiations and acknowledged that the U.S. has followed a policy of sensitivity to the balance of power in the Middle East.

In August, 1969, a fire broke out in the Al-Aksa Mosque in Jerusalem which was under control of the Moslem Religious Trust. An Australian tourist, Michael Denis Rohan, confessed to setting the act of arson and was committed to a mental hospital. Responding to Arab complaints, the Security Council on September 15 voted to condemn Israel in connection with the acts which it linked with political aspects of Jerusalem.

To bolster Egypt's morale following failure of its War of Attrition, a high level conference with Arab leaders was held in Moscow on December 10, 1969. A communique was issued pledging additional arms and the "elimination of the consequences of Israeli aggression."

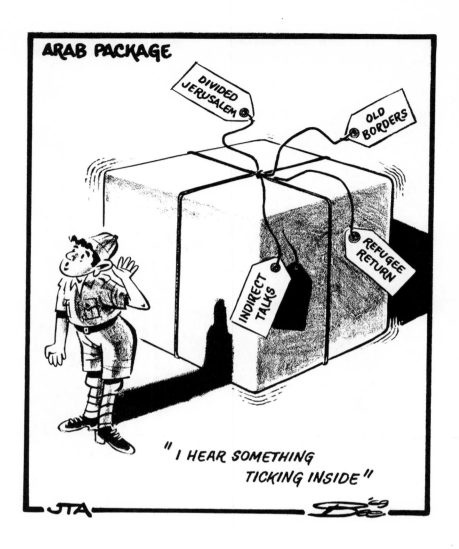

Rumors of talks between Israel and Egypt began to circulate after Egyptian Foreign Minister Mahmoud Riad conferred with Secretary of State William P. Rogers on September 24, 1969. However, Egypt swiftly denied the reports although Riad had hinted that his country was engaged in "Rhodes-type talks."

WELCOME TO THE BENCH!

A TWA plane flying from Rome to Athens was hijacked by terrorists on August 29, 1969, and forced to proceed to Damascus. In violation of international law, two Israeli passengers were held in custody by the Syrians. They were exchanged for 13 Syrians and 58 Egyptian prisoners. In October of the same year, Syria was elected as a member of the Security Council for a two-year term.

To halt the punitive moves into its territory by Israeli troops, Lebanon in late 1969, cleared the terrorists from its frontier areas. However, on October 30, 1969, when the El-Fatah infiltrations resumed, Israel charged these armed groups were operating from Lebanon under the aegis of Syria.

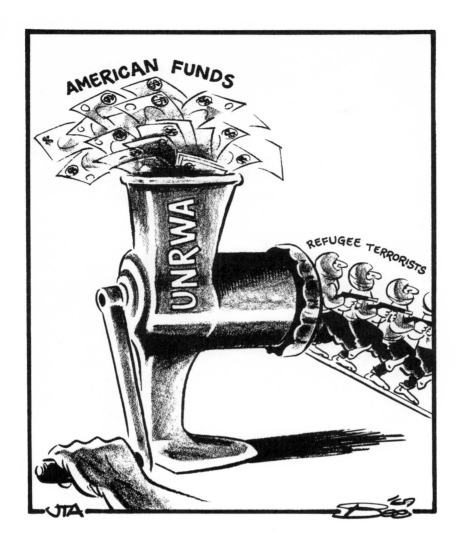

With most of the funds coming from the U.S., the General Assembly allocated on December 11, 1969, an additional $13.8 million to the United Nations Relief and Works Agency (UNRWA) for running the refugee camps. Many of these installations had been used as training grounds for terrorist bands.

A SHINING GALAXY

To cope with continued grave problems facing the state a new Government of national unity was formed, headed by Premier Golda Meir. Included were such well-known figures as Moshe Dayan, Menahem Beigin, Yigal Allon, Pinhas Sapir, Abba Eban, Shimon Peres and Ezer Weizmann.

President Pompidou of France continued to curry favor with the Arabs by selling 120 Mirage jets to Libya in January, 1970. The move was protested by Secretary of State Rogers and segments of the French press and public opinion were also critical. Pompidou's simultaneous announcement of his own modest approach to peace was as one sided as his sale of jets.

In January, 1970, the Supreme Court ruled favorably in the case of the children of Naval Lt. Commander Benjamin Shalit, whose wife is not Jewish. Shalit asserted that a Jew can be defined in terms of nationality alone and, therefore, claimed that his children were Jewish. Halakhah, the Jewish Religious Law, defines a Jew as a child of a Jewish mother or one who undergoes conversion. The Cabinet sought to override the Court's decision.

On February 21, 1970, a Swissair plane bound from Zurich exploded on takeoff. Forty-seven passengers, including fourteen Israelis and six Americans were killed. An Arab terrorist group claimed "credit" for the act. Several European airlines suspended air cargo shipments to Israel. On February 23, Golda Meir made clear that her country "will not acquiesce to any assault on our air routes and will protect them."

During March, 1970, Russian Sam-3 ground-to-air missiles were being installed along the Suez. This posed a grave danger. Israeli pilots who shot down nine MIGs-21's reported that they heard Russian spoken by those flying the enemy planes.

The State celebrated its 22nd anniversary as she stood alone facing the Arab threat backed by the Kremlin. Mrs. Meir asked President Nixon for more military and economic aid to offset massive Russian supplies made available to Egypt.

After a lag, Mideast talks resumed on March 25, 1970, between the United States and the Soviet Union. The latter's position was at once ambiguous and uncompromising. The dialogue gradually faded into nothingness.

The incessant barrage across the Suez continued through late June, with the Russians, at times, flying Egyptian planes. In May, Israeli commandos attacked the Egyptian army base of Bir-Araida, 45 miles inland. In a daring move, they carried back with them a secret Soviet missile installation.

THE BIG CATCH

HUSSEIN

FATAH & CO.

JTA

'70

In June, 1970, as El-Fatah bands continued to operate independently from his territory, King Hussein asserted that his desert country backs the group "with all its resources." In allowing raids across his borders, which brought inevitable counter-attacks, the young monarch virtually became their captive.

136

While Ambassador Jarring in the summer of 1970, resumed his efforts to mediate between both conflicting parties, Russia was engaged in installing missile sites in Egypt. Chief of Staff Hayim Bar-Lev, reported that three Israeli planes were shot down by Russian missiles.

By the summer of 1970, Egypt, realizing that her War of Attrition had failed, accepted a U.S. initiated cease-fire, which went into effect on August 7th. The Soviet Union temporarily slowed down its arms shipments.

THE TROJAN DOVE

ROGERS PLAN

90 DAY TRUCE

Israel agreed to a 90-day cease fire along the Suez Canal in August, 1970, following the reactivation of the Jarring mission. In late 1969, Secretary Rogers outlined a plan which called for the withdrawal from the entire Sinai Peninsula and the turning over of Sharm el-Sheikh to an international force. The plan was opposed by Israel.

139

Prospects for negotiations were stalled when in early September, 1970, Israel discovered that the Egyptians deployed missiles in areas specifically excluded by the cease-fire pact.

On September 12, 1970, Palestine Liberation Front terrorists blew up three hijacked Western airliners. Passengers held as hostages were freed after harrowing negotiations. Red China applauded this act of piracy.

With the sudden death of President Nasser on September 28, 1970, there passed on his dream of uniting the entire Arab world under his domain. The Egyptian people began to pay more attention to their own massive problems.

Celebration of the 25th anniversary of the United Nations was used by Egyptian Foreign Minister Mahmoud Riad on October 16, 1970, as the occasion for denouncing the United States for supporting Israel. He charged the U.S. with having misled Nasser by sending arms to Israel.

On October 15, 1970, acting President Anwar Sadat was elected President of Egypt. The might of the Soviet Union continued to cast a shadow over the land of Nile.

In December, 1970, Senator Henry Jackson termed Rogers' Mideast settlement proposals "shortsighted and ill advised." The formula called for withdrawal from all but "insubstantial parts" of territory occupied in defeating Egypt's aggression in 1967.

On January 5, 1971, Ambassador Jarring resumed the indirect talks between Israel, Egypt and Jordan. The meetings failed when Egypt refused to budge from its rigid position.

On January 15, 1971, Jarring was presented with a 14-point formula by Israel for ending the conflict. The Arab rulers summarily rejected it.

President Sadat continued in February, 1971, to harp on one theme: unconditional withdrawal from "all occupied territories." He assumed the role of a victor refusing to sit at the negotiating table with the "vanquished."

In a resurgence of antisemitism, the Soviet press in May, 1971, charged "Zionists" with instigating plots to subvert regimes in Czechoslovakia and Poland.

The nation celebrated its anniversary in the mood of Masada, the fortress in the Judean wilderness famed for its last stand against the might of the Roman invaders in 70 C.E. Masada became a symbol of the spirit of freedom of the Jewish people.

In May, 1971, Secretary of State Rogers undertook a trip to the Middle East and conferred with President Sadat and with Mrs. Meir. He claimed he found "some narrowing of the gap." Sadat threw cold water on this cautious optimism when he announced that Egypt would insist its troops occupy the entire Sinai.

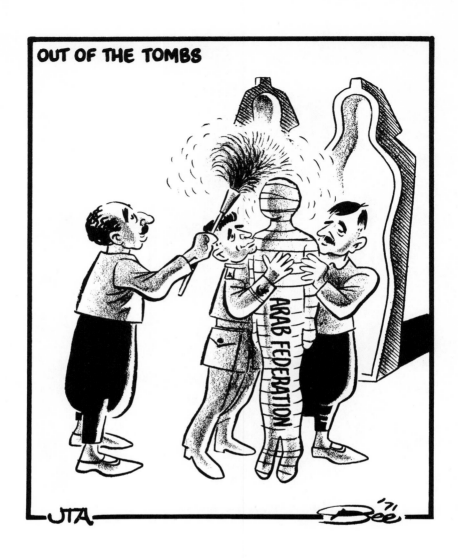

Once again an attempt was made to unify the Arab peoples under Egypt's hegemony. In April, 1971, President Sadat announced formation of a Federation consisting of Egypt, Syria and Libya. He said that it will have "one flag, one anthem and one capital."

Imprisonment of large numbers of Soviet Jews who expressed a desire to emigrate continued through 1971. The awakening of Jewish consciousness among Soviet Jews was growing in spite of the harassment and persecution.

Soviet Russia became even further entrenched within Egypt, as the flow of arms and planes was stepped up in early summer, 1972. Accompanying the deliveries of the weapons were Soviet personnel, many of whom took direct charge of the sophisticated weapons or trained Egyptians to handle them.

In June, 1971, Soviet authorities staged a trial in Kishinev of Jews who applied for permits to emigrate to Israel. They were sentenced to prison terms on charges of subversion. Ironically Kishinev was the scene of one of the bloodiest massacres of Jews by Czarist agents.

On July 15, 1971, the Jordanian army completed its mopping up operations against the terrorists and drove them into the hills. The campaign was launched by King Hussein in September, 1970, from which the "Black September" group took its name.

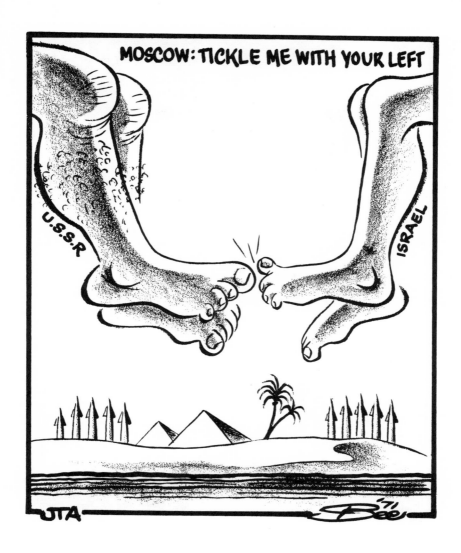

For the first time since 1967, non-Communist leftist Israelis visited Moscow in August, 1971. Noted for their criticism of Israeli foreign policy, the delegation was invited to tour the country by the Soviet Peace Committee

The U.N. General Assembly sessions in September, 1971, were marked by a succession of debates on the Middle East. Members of the Arab-Soviet-African bloc helped bring about a resolution on December 13th, calling for Israel's withdrawal to the 1967 armistice lines.

158

In one of his first addresses at the U.N., Red China's delegate on December 8, 1971, delivered a virulent attack on Israel competing with the Soviet Union for support of the Arab cause. He charged that the U.S. and the U.S.S.R. were "in collusion" to subvert Arab interests.

In the latter part of 1971, President Sadat warned Egyptian troops that war was "at hand." He placed the army on a standby alert and promised action by the end of the year. He also claimed that he had severed contacts with the U.S. for a peaceful solution.

Despite heavy burdens for defense, the people accepted increased taxation, and made other sacrifices to help cover the cost of absorbing 30,000 Soviet immigrants who were expected in 1972.

Israel's agreement on February 2, 1972, to a U.S. proposal for indirect talks on reopening the Suez Canal blunted the edge of Sadat's case. Later Mrs. Meir disclosed that Egypt had turned down previous offers for high level talks.

Rumania's stance toward Israel was more independent than those of other Eastern bloc countries which followed the Kremlin's hard line. After a visit of Golda Meir to President Nicolae Ceausescu, a joint communique was issued that both governments stood for the continuation of efforts towards peaceful settlement of the conflict.

President Nixon's summit meeting with Kremlin leaders in May, 1972, the first visit by an American President to Moscow, was followed with intense interest throughout the world. Israel maintained a watchful eye for any news affecting the Middle East.

Granting Soviet immigrants priority in obtaining modern housing caused discontent among old-time residents. The Government was faced with a delicate internal problem.

On May 9, 1972, three Japanese terrorists who disembarked from an Air France flight from Rome perpetrated a massacre at Lydda Airport. They fired machine guns and lobbed hand grenades into a crowd of some 300, killing 28 and wounding 76. They had been recruited by the Liberation Front.

Toward the end of 1969, Colonel Muammar Qaddafi, who had overthrown the pro-western government of Libya, began to emerge as the newest strongman on the Arab scene. He became an ardent backer of El-Fatah.

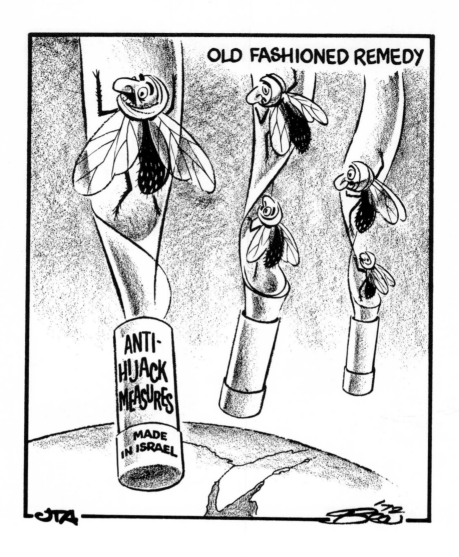

The Lydda Airport outrage and hijackings by terrorists led to a reorganization of the Israeli security system. Measures instituted to maintain security were considered superior to those of other countries.

Continued attacks by raiders from Lebanon provoked Israeli retaliations on June 21 and June 23, 1972. The Security Council again this time shed its lethargy and hastened to condemn Israel by a vote of 13 to 0, with the U.S. and Panama abstaining. The resolution omitted any reference to the terrorist acts against Israel.

In a surprise move on July 18, 1972, President Sadat announced that he had requested the withdrawal of Soviet personnel from Egypt.

The world was stunned by the murder on September 5, 1972, of eleven Israeli athletes at the Olympic Games in Munich by members of the Black September group. "The elite of our sportsmen have died and the Olympic spirit died with them," said Deputy Prime Minister Yigal Allon during the funeral ceremony.

President Sadat's order for the withdrawal of Soviet military personnel reflected his desire to demonstrate independence from the Kremlin. He also harbored the hope of twisting the arm of the Americans who would, in turn, twist the arm of Israelis.

AN EYE OPENER

U.S. VETO

UN SUPPORTERS OF ARAB TERRORISTS

In its second veto cast since the establishment of the United Nations, on September 10, 1972, the U.S. killed a Security Council resolution condemning Israel for its raids into Syria and Lebanon. American Ambassador Bush blocked the one-sided move, so typical of the U.N., when it concerned the Middle East.

On October 3, 1972, the West Germans released three members of the Black September movement who had participated in the murder of Israeli athletes. The government capitulated to demands of Arab hijackers of a Lufthansa plane over Turkey. The Munich assassins were flown to Libya where they were greeted as heroes.

With the 1972 reelection of Richard M. Nixon, Israel and Egypt were all set to resubmit their respective positions designed to win American support.

Despite continued hijackings of airliners, the General Assembly, on December 18, 1972, under pressure voted down a U.S. resolution calling for strong action to cope with this flagrant violation of international law.

176

Arab Foreign Ministers and Defense Chiefs met in Kuwait on November 15, 1972, as a prelude to another Arab summit. However, it ended in failure when King Hussein rejected the demand of the Palestine Liberation group and its supporters to restore their base of operations in Jordan.

The country was aghast in early 1973 that four Sabras, including two former paratroopers, were arrested as members of a Jewish-Arab spy ring operating for Syria. This was the first time since the establishment of the state that native-born Israeli Jews were charged with spying for ideological reasons.

Agreement to end the Vietnam war through direct negotiations in
Paris spurred hope for comparable moves in the Mideast. On
February 18, 1973, Senator Hubert H. Humphrey expressed the view
that resolution of the long and bitter conflict over Vietnam would
have a favorable impact on the Mideast.

Colonel Qaddafi has made large financial grants to African countries as an inducement to sever their relations with Israel. Uganda was the first of five African countries to have done so. The country, which enjoyed very close ties with the Jewish State, announced its support of the Palestinian Liberation Front.

The early part of 1973 brought top ranking emissaries from the Middle East to the White House. First was King Hussein followed by Hafez Ismail, described as the Egyptian Kissinger, and finally Golda Meir. No major changes in U.S. policy emerged. With the gulf between the parties still wide on terms of an over-all settlement, attention in Washington remained focused on an interim pact to open the Suez Canal.

The New York Times disclosed in late March, 1973, that the Nixon Administration agreed to sell Israel additional jet aircraft. Aid for the development of its arms industry to maintain the arms balance in the Middle East was also agreed upon.

Following the American Presidential elections, pro-Arab forces drew on the projected energy crisis as a ploy against Israel. The possible dependence in the future upon the Middle East oil was being used as a means to force a change in the U.S. foreign policy.

Following the resignation of Egyptian Premier Aziz Sidky, Sadat announced that he is assuming the premiership in addition to the presidency and the title of Military Governor of Egypt. He explained this by saying that "we are entering a new stage in total confrontation with Israel." But this move was designed primarily to divert attention from the worsening domestic economic crisis.

184

May 7, 1973. A quarter of a century has passed since the birth of M'dinat Israel. This tiny land achieved international stature far beyond its size, thanks to the courage and fortitude of its people and the support of world Jewry. No nation in history attained so much progress within such a brief span of time. Surrounded by enemies determined to bring about her downfall, she repeatedly extended a hand of peace. It is a country wherein miracles are taken for granted. On this historic anniversary it can be said that Israel is alive, well and flourishing—IN SPITE OF EVERYTHING!